Everybody's Zoo

This book is dedicated to the supporters of *My Kind of Zoo*.
We are honored to have inspired such an outpouring of generosity
in this unprecedented campaign for Lincoln Park Zoo.

Everybody's Zoo

Published by
Lincoln Park Zoo
2001 North Clark Street
Chicago, IL 60614

Telephone: 312-742-2000
www.lpzoo.org

Copyright © 2005
Lincoln Park Zoo

ISBN 0-9769792-0-9

Library of Congress Control Number:
2005929484

Printed and bound in the
United States of America

A destination close to the hearts of all Chicagoans.

This is our visit to Lincoln Park Zoo. We come by busload and stroller, by wagon and hand-in-hand.

Our day is filled with wonder and smiles, picnics and awe, learning and laughter at *Everybody's Zoo*.

Among the wild and the woolly, the scaly and the feathered,
the zoo belongs to all of us.

The Levine Family Polar Bear Plaza

By the bounce of bus seats, children arrive in packs, flocks and gaggles. On this field trip, fun and learning line up together. Our zoo is a living classroom where animals tutor in subjects of the Earth.

Lincoln Park Zoo remains free to the public
with endowment support from the
John D. and Catherine T. MacArthur Foundation
and others.

Beneath our feet the pavement gives way to the grass of the Serengeti. At the end of each path is a

pasture, prairie, jungle or desert. The compass brings animals from every region, near and far.

A journey to the kingdom of animals.

There is the spill of waterfall, the trill of birds, the quiet stance of hippo. This is Africa, where the majestic mingle with the humble, the swift with the slow, and the endangered with the abundant. Such is the grandness of diversity.

Regenstein African Journey was made possible by the extraordinary support of The Regenstein Foundation.

In the species known as family, we rear together on the same planet.

The Aardvark and Meerkat Habitat
McCormick Tribune Foundation
Regenstein African Journey

Across water's grand wilderness goes a **stampede of fish.**
There are glorious migrations everywhere in the waves of nature.

We visit our zoo, but we **wander the world.**

African Savanna
Kovler Family Foundation
Regenstein African Journey

Where animals and people come together, there is a stirring of the mind. Our zoo is a watering

hole for learning, and we are drawn to discovery.

Housed at the William C. Bartholomay Center, the zoo's
conservation and science programs focus on endangered
and threatened species such as the pygmy hippopotamus
at Regenstein African Journey.

There is the tug of responsibility that comes from sharing the world with creatures. We are connected: finger to feather, city to habitat, and conscience to claw. We are together in the same den, nest, burrow and house of Earth.

In a flash of flamingo, the day is dressed for fun.

The Flamingo Habitat
The Women's Board of
The Lincoln Park Zoological Society

In the updraft of grace, a bird takes flight.

If nature has a voice, it is the song and call of birds. Such beauty from beaks!

It is the cadence of all that is right in the world.

The instinct to embrace life is what animals and children have in common.

In the twist and turn of a wooded path, a child's adventure begins. Here are the slap of beaver tail and the trudge of bear. Learning is in the encounter, in the shrieks, giggles and hoots of discovery.

The inspiring generosity of the Pritzker family
made the Pritzker Family Children's Zoo a reality.

The Elizabeth Hubert Malott Black Bear Habitat
Pritzker Family Children's Zoo

The North American River Otter Habitat
McCormick Tribune Foundation
Pritzker Family Children's Zoo

In play, there is a purpose. The job and joy of having fun is for children...and otters.

Life scoots by so fast. Dive into each new day.

Children and animals understand best the touch and tumble of the world. By limb and log, splash and dig, there's exploring to be done! Learning can be found in the ruckus of nature.

The Kresge Foundation is a major funder
of the Pritzker Family Children's Zoo.

The **climb** from childhood should be happy and carefree.

Tree Canopy Climbing Adventure
Polk Bros. Foundation
Pritzker Family Children's Zoo

These are the creatures of prairie and pond, woodland and river. From under red oak and pine,

birch and maple, these are the animals that share our region and our range of home.

The Searle Funds at
The Chicago Community Trust
provided major support for the
Pritzker Family Children's Zoo.

Foreman Pavilion

At the zoo, life is a picnic! We feast under the canopy of shade in the lemonade sun.

Eadie Levy's Landmark Café
Mr. and Mrs. Lawrence F. Levy

In the zoo's backyard, we spread our blankets. On this city quilt of coolers and lawn chairs,

music brings us together like neighbors over fences.

Jammin' at the Zoo

The link of species in the look of an eye.

We leave skyscrapers for the territory of silverbacks, and the slope and plain of city for a

community of chimpanzees. Now we are in a bamboo forest, on the edge of a clearing,

in the mist of an African mountainside.

Regenstein Center for African Apes was
made possible by the unprecedented
generosity of The Regenstein Foundation.

Regenstein Center for African Apes
received major support from
Kay and Jay Proops.

In the presence of gorillas, we find nobility and gentleness.
Magnificence abounds in the quiet fortress of underbrush.

The Bamboo Forest Gorilla Habitat
Kovler Family Foundation
Regenstein Center for African Apes

In the company of chimpanzees, we are curious and connected.
We are glad for the gathering.

In the study of kinship, we compare family trees. Branch by branch, we explore the traits and truths of not-so-distant relatives. At this reunion, there's comfort in the connection.

The Leo S. Guthman Fund
is a significant supporter of
The Lester E. Fisher Center for the
Study and Conservation of Apes.

Preserving wildlife is a sort of precious hoarding. There's hope in the bounty.

The Auxiliary Board Endowed Fund for
Conservation and Science supports the
zoo's field conservation efforts.

Through study and steadfastness, the zoo is a laboratory of our resolve.

Conservation is gratitude and wisdom in action.

Zoo scientists monitor health risks among
animals in the zoo and in the wild as part of
their work at the Davee Center for Epidemiology
and Endocrinology.

We track our humanity through what remains of the wilderness.

At our zoo, we see the prance and sheen of animals that thrive. There is a science to compassion.

We hear the sounds of wellness—the roar, bark, screech and splash of good care.

In the chill and cheer of holiday lights, our spirits are warmed by the hearth of city and a festive night.

ZooLights Presented by ComEd,
an Exelon Company

Bringing the heartland to the heart of the city.

The stalk and crop of countryside unfold before us. Here is the peaceful symmetry of red barn and white fence. We take comfort in knowing the animals by name. In soil and soul, there is something sacred about the family farm.

Farm-in-the-Zoo Presented by John Deere
was created through the generous leadership
support of the John Deere Foundation.

We are students of the hens, the corn and the cows. There's much to learn about the hatch and

harvest of our food and the skills of bounty. We scurry like chicks to the classroom of the barnyard.

The Siragusa Foundation is a major
funder of education initiatives at
Farm-in-the-Zoo Presented by John Deere.

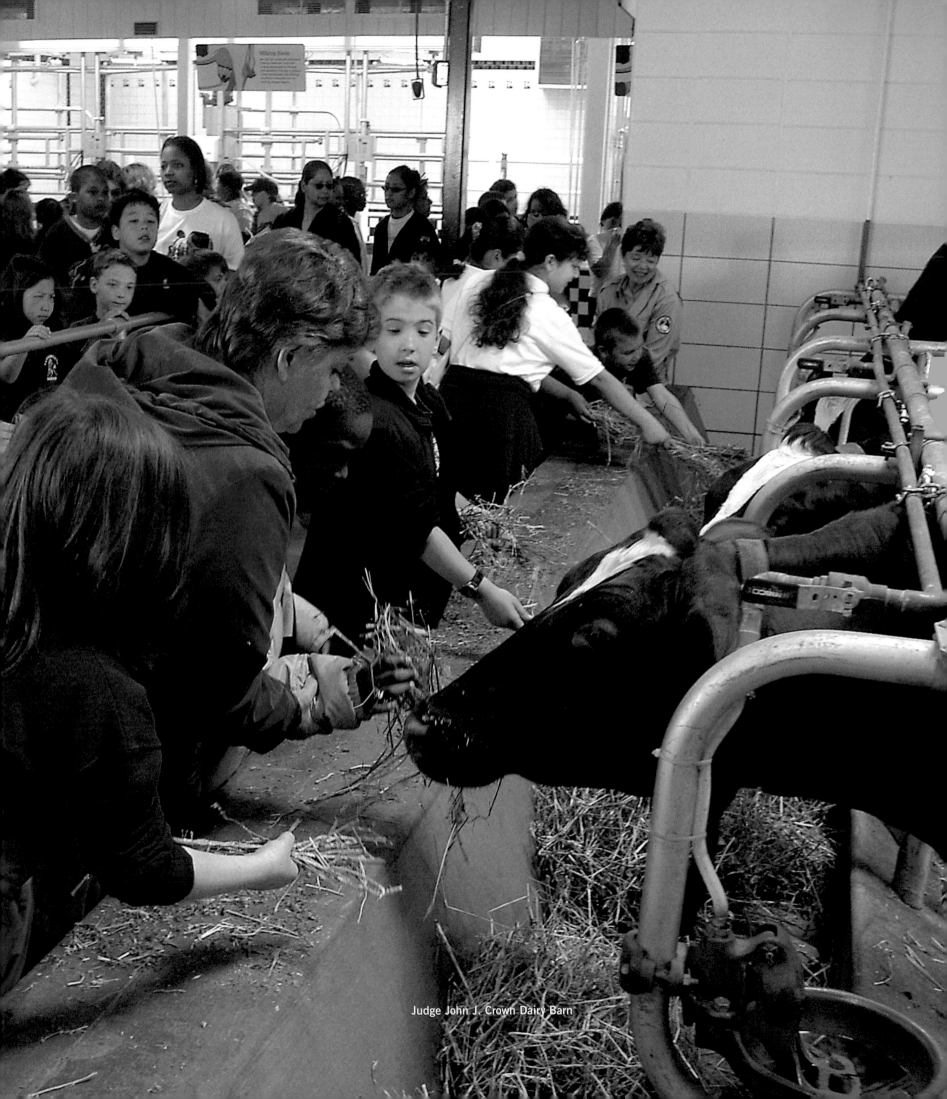

Judge John J. Crown Dairy Barn

The South Pond Project, a local ecology awareness
program, is funded in part by Peoples Energy.

We hear the chatter of crickets and the alto of frogs. What adventures await us at a pond!

We explore like eager ducks on the banks of discovery.

We are urban travelers, and the zoo is our oasis.

Mr. Charles C. Haffner III is a major funder
of the zoo's sculpture and gardens endowment.

The mystery of reptiles uncoils before us.

In the dart of a lizard, we find ourselves in the bog and sand of the cold-blooded.

Here we side-wind through the terrain of the reptiles.

In the **round-and-round** of a busy life, it's good
to have a playful pause.

SBC Endangered Species Carousel

Through the Emily and John Alexander Center for
Applied Population Biology, zoo scientists ensure the
viability of captive and wild animal populations.

With one last zebra bray, we are a joyful herd heading home. Memories are souvenirs for the mind

from our wonderful visit to *Everybody's Zoo*.